J513 M429   MAR 2 2 2006
Mattern, Joanne.
I use math at the game

I USE MATH

I USE MATH AT THE GAME

by Joanne Mattern
Reading consultant: Susan Nations, M.Ed., author/literacy coach/consultant

WR WEEKLY READER
EARLY LEARNING LIBRARY

Please visit our web site at: www.earlyliteracy.cc
For a free color catalog describing Weekly Reader® Early Learning Library's list
of high-quality books, call 1-877-445-5824 (USA) or 1-800-387-3178 (Canada).
Weekly Reader® Early Learning Library's fax: (414) 336-0164.

Library of Congress Cataloging-in-Publication Data available upon request from publisher.
Fax (414) 336-0157 for the attention of the Publishing Records Department.

ISBN 0-8368-4855-1 (lib. bdg.)
ISBN 0-8368-4862-4 (softcover)

This edition first published in 2006 by
Weekly Reader® Early Learning Library
A Member of the WRC Media Family of Companies
330 West Olive Street, Suite 100
Milwaukee, WI 53212 USA

Managing editor: Valerie J. Weber
Art direction: Tammy West
Cover design and page layout: Dave Kowalski
Photo research: Diane Laska-Swanke
Photographer: Gregg Andersen

Printed in the United States of America

1 2 3 4 5 6 7 8 9 09 08 07 06 05

Note to Educators and Parents

Reading is such an exciting adventure for young children! They are beginning to integrate their oral language skills with written language. To encourage children along the path to early literacy, books must be colorful, engaging, and interesting; they should invite the young reader to explore both the print and the pictures.

I Use Math is a new series designed to help children read about using math in their everyday lives. In each book, young readers will explore a different activity and solve math problems along the way.

Each book is specially designed to support the young reader in the reading process. The familiar topics are appealing to young children and invite them to read — and reread — again and again. The full-color photographs and enhanced text further support the student during the reading process.

In addition to serving as wonderful picture books in schools, libraries, homes, and other places where children learn to love reading, these books are specifically intended to be read within an instructional guided reading group. This small group setting allows beginning readers to work with a fluent adult model as they make meaning from the text. After children develop fluency with the text and content, the book can be read independently. Children and adults alike will find these books supportive, engaging, and fun!

— Susan Nations, M.Ed., author, literacy coach, and consultant in literacy development

I am going to my first baseball game with Dad, my sister, and my brother. These are great seats! We are sitting close to the field.

How many of us are there?

5

There are players from each team on the field. The coaches and umpires are on the field, too.

How many people on the baseball field are wearing red shirts?

7

There are nine innings in most baseball games. The scoreboard shows the score in each inning.

After four innings, how many innings will be left to play?

The batter's job is to hit the ball. If he swings and misses the ball three times, he is out.

This batter has swung twice and missed. How many more swings does he get before he is out?

10

11

The scoreboard shows how many runs each team scores. It also shows what inning it is.

How many runs have the Twins scored so far?

12

AT BAT **BALL** **STRIKE** **OUT** **H/E**

	1	2	3	4	5	6	7	8	9	RUNS	HITS	ERRORS
GUEST												
TWINS												

MIKE
REDMOND

ANIMATED DISPLAYS

13

I am so thirsty. My dad gave me ten dollars to buy a cold drink. The cold drink cost three dollars.

How much change will I get back?

Now the other team
has scored some runs.
The game is tied.

How many runs has the guest team scored?

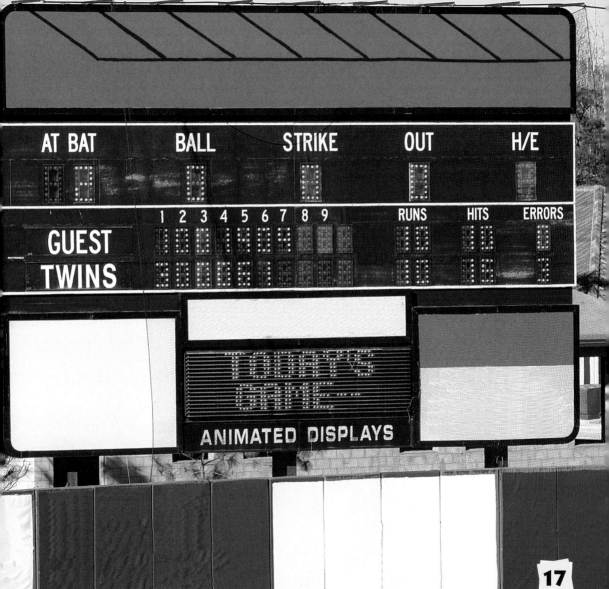

AT BAT BALL STRIKE OUT H/E

1 2 3 4 5 6 7 8 9 RUNS HITS ERRORS

GUEST
TWINS

ANIMATED DISPLAYS

17

Each inning has two halves. After the first half of the seventh inning, everyone stands up to stretch. I like to stretch and sing along with the songs.

One half of the seventh inning is over. How many halves are left in this inning?

We got out of the game at 3:00.
It will take us a half hour to get home.

What time will we get home?

Glossary

coaches — people who train players

innings — parts of a baseball game

runs — a score in baseball

scored — made a point in a game

strike — to swing and miss the ball

team — a group of people who play together

tied — when two teams have the same score

umpire — a person who makes sure the game is played fairly

Answers

Page 4 – 4

Page 6 – 9

Page 8 – 5

Page 10 – 1

Page 12 – 10

Page 14 – $7

Page 16 – 10

Page 18 – 1

Page 20 – 3:30

For More Information

Books

Baseball. Cynthia Fitterer Klingel
   (Child's World)
Counting: Follow That Fish! Math Monsters (series).
   John Burnstein (Weekly Reader® Early
   Learning Library)
My Baseball Book. Gail Gibbons
   (HarperCollins)
Nick Plays Baseball. Rachel Isadora
   (Putnam)

Websites

Kids Domain Baseball Fun
www. Kidsdomain.com/sports/baseball
This site features online games, coloring pages,
clip art, and downloads about baseball

Math Baseball
www.funbrain.com/math
Answer math problems to score runs in this online
baseball learning game

Index

About the Author

Joanne Mattern is the author of more than 130 books for children. Her favorite subjects are animals, history, sports, and biography. Joanne lives in New York State with her husband, three young daughters, and three crazy cats.